▲ LifeGuide®FAMILY
▲ Bible Studies
for Parents and Kids to Do Together

God's Great Invention

18 Studies on Liking Who God Made You to Be

With Notes for Parents

Linda R. Joiner

General Editor
James C. Galvin, Ed.D.

InterVarsity Press
Downers Grove, Illinois 60515, USA

Crossway Books
Leicester, UK

InterVarsity Press
P.O. Box 1400, Downers Grove, IL 60515, USA

Crossway Books
38 De Montfort Street, Leicester LE1 7GP, UK

InterVarsity Press®, U.S.A., is the book-publishing division of InterVarsity Christian Fellowship®, a student movement active on campus at hundreds of universities, colleges and schools of nursing in the United States of America, and a member movement of the International Fellowship of Evangelical Students. For information about local and regional activities, write Public Relations Dept., InterVarsity Christian Fellowship, 6400 Schroeder Rd., P.O. Box 7895, Madison, WI 53707-7895.

LifeGuide® is a registered trademark of InterVarsity Christian Fellowship.

All Scripture quotations are from the International Children's Bible, New Century Version, *copyright © 1986, 1988, 1994 by Word Publishing, Dallas, Texas 75039. Used by permission.*

This book was developed exclusively for InterVarsity Press by The Livingstone Corporation. James C. Galvin, Daryl J. Lucas and Linda R. Joiner, project staff.

Cover photograph: Michael Goss

Activities: Deborah Peska-Keiser

USA ISBN 0-8308-1117-6
UK ISBN 1-85684-130-8

Printed in the United States of America ♾

26	25	24	23	22	21	20	19	18	17	16	15	14	13	12	11	10	9	8	7	6	5	4	3	2	1
17	16	15	14	13	12	11	10	09	08	07	06	05	04	03	02	01	00	99	98	97	96	95

CONTENTS

Welcome to LifeGuide® Family Bible Studies

If you have ever wondered how to make Bible study fun for kids, you will be delighted with this series of study guides. It provides an easy way to study the Bible with a young child or all together as a family. LifeGuide® Family Bible Studies were created especially for families with children ages 4-12. The simple, friendly format makes it easy for adults and children to finish together in just fifteen minutes a day. The material is undated so you can work through the guide at your own pace and according to your family's schedule.

Getting the Most from LifeGuide® Family Bible Studies

Understanding the format used in this series allows you to adapt each lesson to the needs of your family. Each lesson includes a passage from the Bible to read together, questions to discuss, fun activities and a prayer. You can spend more time on some sections and less on others, depending on the age and needs of your child.

Opening. When you sit down together, you need some way to focus your child's attention. The introductory paragraphs start with the child's frame of reference and leads him or her to the truth presented in the Bible passage. Often, the opening includes a question to ask your child or family so that you can find out more about what they are thinking. The opening also creates interest in the Bible verses for that lesson. If your child can read, have him or her read both the opening and the Bible text.

Bible Reading. The translation used in these study guides is the *International Children's Bible.* Having the text reprinted in the study guides makes it easy to use, and also allows children to use highlighters and colored pencils in their study of the Scriptures without fear of ruining a Bible. If you prefer, you can easily use other Bibles in conjunction with the lesson. Either way, the Bible reading usually generates questions.

Discussion Questions. Each lesson includes several questions to discuss to deepen your understanding of the passage. Some of the questions will require your child to look for the answers in the Bible reading. Others will help your child to think about how the truths apply to life.

✎More difficult questions for older children are marked with a pencil.

Activity. Each study guide contains a variety of fun paper and pencil activities such as simple crossword puzzles, mazes and decoding games. These activities can help motivate kids to complete the lesson each day. If you are sharing one study guide with several children, you can take turns letting each child complete the puzzle for the day.

Prayer. The main point of the lesson is also expressed in the prayer that you and your child can pray

Prayer. The main point of the lesson is also expressed in the prayer that you and your child can pray together. You can add more to each prayer as appropriate. But your child may not want to stop there.

Bonus. We have also included an active learning experience for a longer session when you have time and your child wants to do more. Or, you may want to save it for another day. The bonus activity provides additional reinforcement for the main point of the lesson.

Notes to Parents. You will find notes conveniently placed in the margins of each lesson rather than in a separate leader's guide. These notes provide practical help as you study the Bible together.

Studying the Bible with Children

You will find it useful to keep developmental differences in mind as you study the Bible together. After all, children are not miniature adults, and they would not learn well from Bible study approaches suitable for adults. The following chart illustrates some of the characteristics of children at different ages and relates them to Bible study. Which have you noticed in your own child?

Ages	Characteristics of Children	Implications for Bible Study
4-5 early childhood	In general, children this age: • learn by asking questions • usually have many fears • sometimes confuse make-believe with reality • have a growing sense of right and wrong • have a relatively short attention span (5-10 minutes)	As you teach your child: • allow them to ask questions, and answer them patiently • discuss God's protection • don't be surprised if Bible stories get mixed up with pretend stories • distinguish between right and wrong • don't expect to finish each lesson in one sitting
6-8 middle childhood	• are emergent readers; some are fluent readers • think concretely and literally; abstractions tend to be difficult • are able to memorize information easily • thrive on approval from their parents	• use this as an opportunity to practice reading skills • discuss the here and now, avoiding abstractions • make a game out of memorizing a few short verses from a study guide • praise and encourage as much as possible
9-11 later childhood	• are beginning to reason more logically • want to be independent learners • eagerly enter into competitive activities • have many questions about Christianity	• use the questions marked with a pencil, which are more challenging to answer • let your child set the pace and read as you facilitate • try not to have a winner and loser of the Bible study • help your child find answers to his or her questions in the Bible

With so many differences between older and younger children, you will have to adapt some lessons and skip certain activities. You may want to encourage the older children to help the younger ones. Think of these lessons as a helpful guide. Answering your child's questions may ultimately be more important than finishing a lesson. The following guidelines will help you adapt the lessons to meet the needs of children of different ages.

Using These Studies as a Family

You can use these studies to guide your family devotions. If you do, the biggest challenge will be keeping the attention and interest of both younger and older children at the same time. One useful technique for leading the discussion is to ask the question, then allow the children to answer one at a time, starting with the youngest and moving in order to the oldest. This way the younger children have a chance to talk, and the older children have a chance to add their answers. Don't let one child be critical of another child's answer. Parents can join in the fun, too. Your children will be interested in the personal applications that you see in the lesson.

You may have to change some of the wording in the lessons. When using the prayer as a family, change the *me* and *my* to *us* and *our*. Also, you may not want to do the puzzle as a group. Above all, keep it fun. Try to end with a snack or treat of some kind. You may find that your family wants to work through the entire series.

Using These Studies with a Younger Child

Younger children have boundless energy and short attention spans. Keep each lesson short and sweet. You may not be able to finish every lesson in one sitting; if so, just finish up the next day. Make use of the bonus activities at the end because these are more active in nature.

In general, don't use the questions marked with a pencil.

Some of the puzzles are designed to appeal to younger children, and some to older children. Feel free to skip the puzzles that seem too difficult.

Allow your child to ask questions at any point in the lesson. Sometimes the questions may seem endless, but that is a sign that your child is learning. Praise and encourage your child as much as possible during the study.

If your child cannot read, read the prayer one phrase at a time and have the child repeat it after you. Encourage your child to express his or her feelings to God in prayer, and also to make requests to his or her Heavenly Father.

If your child is an emergent reader, make the Bible study a fun experience by letting him or her circle important words or use a highlighter (just like Mom and Dad). Colored pens and pencils can add excitement to the lesson. Make Bible study an adventure.

Using These Studies with an Older Child

Older children don't want to be treated like little kids. They will quickly spot the parts of each lesson intended for younger children. If this happens, don't argue. Simply let them know that they will be treated differently, that they don't have to do all the parts of every lesson, and that this study should be very *easy* for them to complete.

In general, skip the bonus activities, because these are primarily for younger children. You can let your child choose whether or not to complete the puzzle in each lesson. Some of them will be far too easy, and some will be a challenge. The discussion questions marked with a pencil are more difficult and are for older children. Don't skip these. You may want to keep a concordance and Bible dictionary handy for questions that come up along the way.

Older children can be challenged to begin a personal devotional life. If appropriate for your child, consider letting him or her work alone on the study as a step toward developing a personal quiet time. Discuss the lesson with your child after he or she has answered all the questions.

The LifeGuide® Family Bible Studies

The entire series includes eight different study guides. Each study guide contains 18 lessons on a particular topic. Start with the topics that would be most interesting to your family.

Super Bible Heroes. The Bible is full of people who did great things, heroic things. But they really aren't very much bigger or stronger or braver than you. Reading their stories, you'll see how God can help you do what seems impossible on your own.

Grown Up on the Inside. Just as food, exercise and rest help us grow up on the outside, the Bible shows us how to grow up on the inside. It shows us how to practice being loyal, humble, honest, respectful and caring—everything that God knows will make us happy and healthy.

Fruit-Filled. Everybody has a favorite: blueberry Pop-Tarts, apple pie, Jell-O with bananas in it. The Bible tells us how we can be filled with God's favorite fruits: love, joy, peace, patience, kindness, goodness, faithfulness, gentleness and self-control.

Good Choice, Bad Choice. Every day we make choices: Will I watch TV or play outside after supper? What will I do when someone makes me mad? The Bible shows us how God helped other people make decisions—and how he will help us.

Jesus Loves Me. Jesus is the friend who never disappoints us or moves to another city. He is the friend who always understands our problems, who always has time to listen and help. The Bible shows us many ways Jesus loves us and helps us see his care in the things that happen to us every day.

The Friendship Factory. Friends make life fun. They help us learn, grow and know God better. And what the Bible says about friendship can help us be better friends to the people we know.

Wisdom Workshop. King Solomon wanted to be wise. So he asked God for wisdom. In the book of Proverbs he tells what God helped him learn about wisdom—and what you can learn too.

God's Great Invention. God made comets and colors and kangaroos. But his greatest invention is people—people like you. The Bible shows how God made you different from everyone else, with gifts and talents to make your own special mark on his world.

No matter which study guide you begin with, you will be introducing your child to the exciting challenge of studying God's Word and planting the seeds for a lifetime habit of personal Bible study.

James C. Galvin
General Editor

1

You Are Made in God's Image

Fingerprints are amazing! No one in the world has a fingerprint exactly like yours! Every single person has a pattern all his or her own. What do you notice about your fingerprint?

Even though our fingerprints are all different, all of us are made in God's image. That means that in some way we are like him. He also gave us responsibility for taking care of other parts of his creation. God showed how much he cared about us from the moment he made us!

Bible Reading

27So God created human beings in his image. In the image of God he created them. He created them male and female. 28God blessed them and said, "Have many children and grow in number. Fill the earth and be its master. Rule over the fish in the sea and over the birds in the sky. Rule over every living thing that moves on the earth." . . .

31God looked at everything he had made, and it was very good. (Genesis 1:27-28, 31)

Discussion

1. What instructions did God give to the people he created (verse 28)?

2. In short, God made us like himself. Although this is a question to occupy theologians, it can be answered in part by the passage. God has made us like himself by giving us the ability and responsibility to rule over the animal world. Our ability to have children also mirrors God's original creative act.

2. What do you think it means that we are created in God's image (verses 27-28)?

3. What did God say about the people he had made (verse 31)?

4. The questions marked with a pencil are more difficult and intended for older children.

✎4. What is "very good" about the way God made you (verse 31)?

✎5. How does the rest of God's creation show God's love for us?

6. How can you help to take care of God's creation this week?

7. How does it make you feel to know that you were created by God?

Activity

God made us complete in his image. Find the only one of the parrots that is complete.

Prayer

Dear God,
Thank you for making me in your image. Thank you for trusting people to take care of your creation. Help me to be glad to be who you made me to be.
In Jesus' name, amen.

Bonus

Here's how you can get a look at your fingerprint. Use a rolling pin or cardboard tube to make some clay or play-dough very smooth and flat. Then firmly press your index finger into the clay. Lift your finger and look at the print you have made. Ask your parent to make a print next to yours. Notice how they are different. Together, thank God for all the different people he has made in his image.

If you have one, you can use a stamp pad with washable ink and white paper.

2

You Are Special Because God Made You

What do you know about a baby before it is born? Before a baby is born, we do not know very much about him or her. Only after the baby is born can we see how big he or she is, the color of hair and eyes, and the way the baby's voice sounds. Then we can say that we are getting to know that baby. But God knows all about that baby *before* he or she is born.

There was never a time when God didn't know all about you. The writer of Psalm 139 praised God for caring so much about him.

Bible Reading

[13]You made my whole being. You formed me in my mother's body. [14]I praise you because you made me in an amazing and wonderful way. What you have done is wonderful. I know this very well. [15]You saw my bones being formed as I took shape in my mother's body. When I was put together there, [16]you saw my body as it was formed. All the days planned for me were written in your book before I was one day old. (Psalm 139:13-16)

Allow your child to answer the questions.

Your child may know that medical tests can reveal certain information about an unborn baby. But even doctors can't find out everything they would like to know until the baby is born.

Discussion

1. How did your life begin (verse 13)?

2. You may want to answer this question from the perspective of a parent.

2. What amazes you about the way God creates a new life (verse 14)?

3. What did God see happening when no one else could see (verses 15-16)?

4. When did God start making plans for your life (verse 16)?

5. How does it make you feel to know that God could see you before you were born (verses 15-16)?

✎6. If God knew everything about you before you were born, how much do you think he knows about you now?

✎7. What does it mean that God made your "whole being" (verse 13)?

Activity

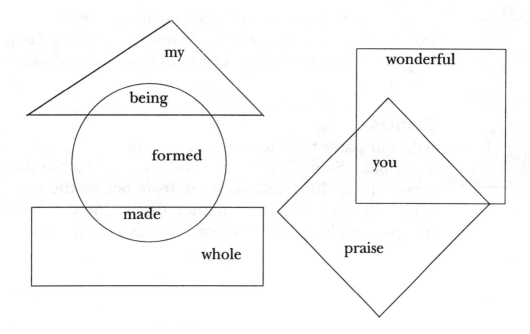

You will uncover a message from the Bible reading by answering the questions below and filling in the answer in the space.

What is in the square and in the diamond?	What is in the circle and in the rectangle?	What is in the triangle but not in the circle?	What is not in the circle but is in the rectangle?	What is in the triangle and in the circle?

Prayer

Dear Jesus,
Thank you that you have known me longer than anyone in the world. Thank you that you made my whole being. Help me to be glad to be myself because you care so much about me.
Amen.

Bonus

Ask your parent to show you pictures of yourself when you were a tiny baby. Some families even have fuzzy, black-and-white pictures, called ultrasound pictures, from before the baby is born. What did you look like? Together, thank God that he was watching over you long before those pictures were taken!

God Lives in You!

Part of taking care of our things is keeping them safe. When something is very special to you, where do you keep it? Sometimes the places where we store things are very ordinary. In Bible times, clay jars were used to store many things: special kinds of food or drink or water for cleaning. Like many of our containers, they could break or get dirty. These verses tell how we are like those clay jars.

Allow your child to answer the question.

Bible Reading

[5]We do not preach about ourselves. But we preach that Jesus Christ is Lord; and we preach that we are your servants for Jesus. [6]God once said, "Let the light shine out of the darkness!" And this is the same God who made his light shine in our hearts. He gave us light by letting us know the glory of God that is in the face of Christ. [7]We have this treasure from God. But we are only like clay jars that hold the treasure. This shows that this great power is from God, not from us. [8]We have troubles all around us, but we are not defeated. We do not know what to do, but we do not give up. [9]We are persecuted, but God does not leave us. We are hurt sometimes, but we are not destroyed. (2 Corinthians 4:5-9)

Discussion

1. What is the treasure we have from God (verses 5-7)?

1. The treasure is the good news about Jesus (refer to verses 5 and 6.)

2. How are we like clay jars (verse 7)?

2. Help your child to see the good news that God uses ordinary people. We are like containers for God to use. It is his power, not our own efforts, that brings him praise.

3. If you are a "clay jar" for God, what does he keep in you?

3. The implication from the surrounding verses is that we contain the power of the Gospel.

4. Why don't Christians give up when bad things happen to them (verses 8-9)?

5. How does it make you feel to know that you are a container for God's treasure?

✎6. Why is it good for people to know that the power we carry is God's power and not our own (verse 7)?

✎7. How does God help us with our troubles?

Activity

Draw a line connecting the dots between numbers 1 and 16 and between the letters that are the same. You will find something that gives off light like God's love shining in your heart.

Prayer

Dear Jesus,
Thank you for making me a container for your treasure. Thank you for showing your great power in my life. Help me to remember that I am special because I am a container for the message of Jesus.
Amen.

Bonus

Try this activity to see how what we keep in a container can make the container seem more special. Find two clear water glasses. Fill one with plain water. Then fill the other and add a few drops of your favorite color of food coloring. Stir the coloring into the water. Then hold both glasses up to the light. What is special about the colored water? Which glass seems prettiest to you now? How is this like Jesus coming into a person's life?

Your Body Is a Home for God's Spirit

Allow your child to answer the questions.

Everyone likes to have a place to call home. We take care of our homes by cleaning them. We decorate them in ways that we especially like. What is special to you about your home?

God told the people in the Old Testament to build a temple that would be like a "home" for God and a place to meet with him. They took a long time to build it, and they made it very beautiful. Of course, God is everywhere. We cannot contain him in a place that we make. But God was honored by the people who made this special place. After Jesus returned to heaven, he sent the Holy Spirit to live in us. Now, every Christian is like a temple where God's Spirit lives.

Bible Reading

[19]You should know that your body is a temple for the Holy Spirit. The Holy Spirit is in you. You have received the Holy Spirit from God. You do not own yourselves. [20] You were bought by God for a price. So honor God with your bodies. (1 Corinthians 6:19-20)

Discussion

1. In what way are our bodies like the temple that Israel built for worshiping God (verse 19)?

2. Because you know your body is a home for the Holy Spirit, how should you treat it ?

3. Who owns our bodies if we are Christians (verses 19-20)?

4. What price did God pay for us (verse 20)?

5. What does it mean for you to honor God with your body (verse 20)?

✎6. What are some ways that Christians should *not* treat their bodies because their bodies are temples for the Holy Spirit?

✎7. What can you do to remind yourself that the Holy Spirit lives in you?

4. This question can lead to some humorous answers. Be sure to enjoy them. If your child is not accustomed to hearing the gospel in this way, explain that all people have sinned. When we sin, we become slaves to sin. (In that sense, we don't even "own ourselves" before we accept Christ.) The price to free us from sin and allow us to belong to God was the sacrifice of the Lamb of God, Jesus, who never sinned. God sent his Son in the form of a man and allowed him to die so that he could "buy us back" from our slavery to sin.

Activity

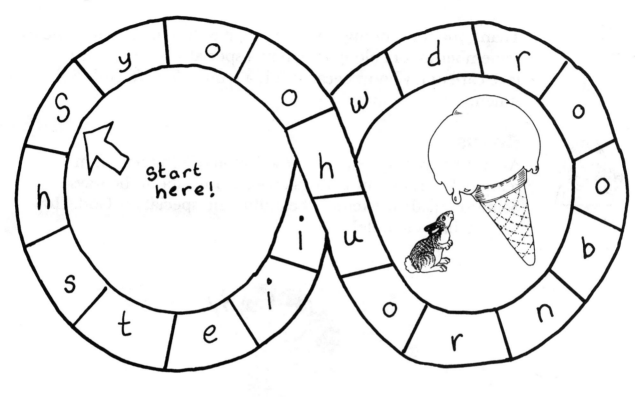

Start here!

S y o o h i i e t s h

w d r o o b n r o u h

___ ___ ___ ___ ___ ___ ___ ___ **God** ___ ___ ___ ___ ___

___ ___ ___ ___ ___ ___ ___ ___ ___ ___

Start at the arrow and go twice around the figure eight, writing every other letter in the blanks. You will complete the sentence and discover something from the Bible reading.

Prayer

Dear Jesus,
Thank you for sending the Holy Spirit to live in me. Help me to remember that I belong to you in a special way. Help me to take care of my body, because it is a temple for the Holy Spirit. Amen.

Bonus

Ask your parent to read the description of King Solomon's temple. It is found in 1 Kings 6:14-35. Talk about the ways Solomon made the temple beautiful and special for God. How are you like a temple?

5

God Takes Care of You

Allow your child to answer the question.

One of the most important jobs your parent has is taking care of you. Parents do this because they love their children. What are some of the ways your parent takes care of you? While your parent is taking care of you, God is watching over both of you. Even when you are grown up, God will be there to take care of you.

King David in the Old Testament had taken care of sheep when he was a boy. He knew all the things a shepherd had to do to make sure the sheep stayed safe, healthy and happy. When he thought about God's care for him, he thought about God as the shepherd and himself as a sheep.

Bible Reading

[1]The Lord is my shepherd. I have everything I need. [2]He gives me rest in green pastures. He leads me to calm water. [3]He gives me new strength. For the good of his name, he leads me on paths that are right. [4]Even if I walk through a very dark valley, I will not be afraid because you are with me. Your rod and your walking stick comfort me. (Psalm 23:1-4)

Discussion

1. Why is it good that God is our shepherd (verse 1)?

2. Why do sheep like to have green pastures and calm water (verse 2)?

3. What does God do for us when we are tired, or when we are not sure which way to go (verse 3)?

4. Explain to your child that a shepherd uses his rod to keep the sheep from straying off the path. A good shepherd does not hit the sheep with his rod. When the sheep feel that firm touch, they know that the shepherd is close by and they will not fall into any harm.

4. How does God's guiding hand help us not to be afraid (verse 4)?

5. In what ways has God made sure that you are taken care of?

✎6. Why is it dangerous for a sheep to be without a shepherd?

✎7. Why are you glad that God cares for both children *and* grownups?

Activity

mechanic

Florist

cobbler

rancher

farmer

Shepherd

baker

God watches over you. Match each picture with someone who watches over it.

Prayer

Dear God,
Thank you for making me the way you did. Thank you for caring for me the way a shepherd cares for sheep. Help me to love you and follow you always.
In Jesus' name, amen.

Bonus

On a large sheet of paper, draw a picture of a flock of sheep living in the open. Draw one of the dangers that the sheep might face. Then draw the shepherd who is there to protect them. Explain your picture to your parent and talk about how God cares for you.

6

Allow your child to answer the question.

God Gives You Everything You Need

Worry is not a pleasant feeling. When we worry, we think about bad things that might happen. Worrying makes us feel scared. What have you been worried about lately?

God knew that everyone tends to worry. But he made us his children, and he is always watching over us. So there is really no need for us to worry. Jesus said that God will take good care of us.

Bible Reading

^{25}[Jesus said] "So I tell you, don't worry about the food you need to live. And don't worry about the clothes you need for your body. Life is more important than food. And the body is more important than clothes. ^{26}Look at the birds in the air. They don't plant or harvest or store food in barns. But your heavenly Father feeds the birds. And you know that you are worth much more than the birds." (Matthew 6:25-26)

Discussion

1. Do you tend to worry more about food or clothing? Why (verse 25)?

2. How does God give us food and clothes?

3. Why are people worth more to God than birds (verse 26)?

4. How can we learn to trust God more for the things we need every day, like food and clothing?

5. How valuable are you to God (verse 26)?

6. What can you do the next time you feel like worrying about your food and clothing?

7. How does knowing that God values you more than the plants and animals help you to be glad to be who you are?

1. Children have strong likes and dislikes about foods, and they sometimes begin to feel peer pressure with regard to clothing styles at an early age. Take this opportunity to discuss with your child what is really important. We can fall into the trap of always wanting more and better things, or we can cultivate a sense of gratitude for the gift of life itself.

2. Human beings can be misled into thinking that they are meeting their own daily needs because planning and toil go into the way we get our food. The birds, on the other hand, are dependent on what they find from day to day. Although people will always plant and harvest, store, buy and prepare food, they should remember that God is the real source of all that we need.

3. This can lead to an interesting conversation with your child. Ultimately, human beings are made in the image of God and animals are not (Genesis 1:24-26). But God also wants us to be kind to our animals (Proverbs 12:10).

Activity

food	You	life	are	plant
worth	harvest	much	clothes	more
than	the	store	birds	live

Cross out the squares that contain the following. When the squares left are read across from top to bottom, you will find a message from the Bible reading.

1. Two things from the Bible reading that Jesus does not want us to worry about.

2. Two words that begin with the letter *L*.

3. Three things that Jesus said the birds do not do (see verse 26).

Prayer

Dear Lord,
Thank you for valuing me more highly than any of the wonderful animals that you have created. Thank you that you have promised to take care of me just like you take care of them. Help me to trust you and be glad for who I am.
In Jesus' name, amen.

Bonus

With your parent, find a place in your yard or a nearby park where you can watch the birds. Find a place to sit and be very still for at least ten minutes. Quietly point out any birds you see and notice what they are doing. You will find that the birds are busy all the time looking for the food and water they need to live. Notice the ways that God provides for them.

7

Allow your child to answer the questions.

Jesus Has a Special Love for Children

Children are usually treated with special care and concern. But sometimes children are ignored. Also, they are not allowed to do certain things until they get older. What do you like about being a child? What do you dislike?

Some people in Jesus' time especially wanted their children to meet Jesus. Others thought that Jesus was too busy to be bothered with little children. Let's find out how Jesus treated the children.

Bible Reading

[13]Then the people brought their little children to Jesus so that he could put his hands on them and pray for them. When his followers saw this, they told the people to stop bringing their children to Jesus. [14]But Jesus said, "Let the little children come to me. Don't stop them, because the kingdom of heaven belongs to people who are just like these children." (Matthew 19:13-14)

Discussion

1. Why did people bring their little children to Jesus (verse 13)?

2. What did Jesus' followers tell the people with the children (verse 13)?

3. What did Jesus do when he saw his followers turning the children away (verse 14)?

4. While children are living through this stage of their lives, you may need to help them come to an awareness of what it was that Jesus was commending. Jesus saw that the openness and receptivity that comes naturally to children is what is required of anyone who wants to come to salvation in him.

4. What was it about the little children that made them special to Jesus?

5. What do you like best about the way Jesus talked about children?

✎6. What do you think Jesus prayed for the children who came to him?

✎7. What are some ways that parents bring children to Jesus today?

Activity

USEBECA   ___ ___ ___ ___ ___ ___ ___

VHEEAN   ___ ___ ___ ___ ___ ___

ITLETL   ___ ___ ___ ___ ___ ___

OLDT   ___ ___ ___ ___

SANDH   ___ ___ ___ ___ ___

YRAP   ___ ___ ___ ___

ELT   ___ ___ ___

HENW   ___ ___ ___ ___

Unscramble the letters on the left to reveal words from the Bible reading. The word that is formed in the column down the middle will tell you who the kingdom of heaven belongs to.

Prayer

Dear Jesus,
Thank you for making me the way you did. Thank you for loving children and making time for them. Help me always to be eager to come to you and to talk to you.
Amen.

Bonus

Ask your parent to pretend to be one of Jesus' followers who wanted to turn away the parents and their children. See if you can explain *why* Jesus wanted to see the children. Together, thank Jesus for loving children so much.

8

Allow your child to answer the question.

God Speaks to the Boy Samuel

We think of people as important for many reasons. They might know valuable information, like doctors or lawyers. They might make important decisions, like government leaders. Others might be famous. What important people can you name?

God does not consider people important for the same reasons we usually do. God looks at people's hearts, not at how strong or smart or popular they are. Samuel was a young boy who lived in the temple and helped the priests. Read this story to find out why a young boy was very important to God.

Bible Reading

[8]The Lord called Samuel for the third time. Samuel got up and went to Eli. He said, "I am here. You called me."

Then Eli realized the Lord was calling the boy. [9]So he told Samuel, "Go to bed. If he calls you again, say, 'Speak, Lord. I am your servant, and I am listening.' " . . .

[10]The Lord came and stood there. He called as he had before. He said, "Samuel, Samuel!"

Samuel said, "Speak, Lord. I am your servant, and I am listening." (1 Samuel 3:8-10)

Discussion

1. How did Samuel show that he was obedient to the grownups around him (verse 8)?

2. Why didn't Samuel know that the voice calling his name was God (verses 8-9)?

3. What did Samuel say to the Lord when the Lord came to talk to him (verse 10)?

4. Why would God choose to talk to a little boy?

4. With so many people in Israel unreceptive to God's voice and disobedient to his laws, God needed someone who would wholeheartedly obey him. In 1 Samuel 2, God had sent a prophet to let Eli the priest know that God was displeased by the sinful behavior of his family. Later, in 1 Samuel 3, God tells Samuel that he will judge Eli and his family for their sins.

5. How does the story of God and Samuel make you glad to be a child who is learning about God?

✎6. How can you become a better listener to God's Word?

✎7. How can you show God that you are ready to do what he asks?

Activity

S	A	M	U	E	L	I	N	G	L	E	D
P	E	N	S	E	R	V	A	N	T	E	W
E	L	I	T	I	M	E	L	O	V	E	E
A	G	P	O	M	A	B	E	D	O	W	N
K	P	R	O	I	S	E	O	L	C	E	T
R	H	A	D	E	K	L	A	Y	O	E	O
D	D	Y	C	A	L	L	I	N	G	R	E
L	I	S	T	E	N	I	N	G	E	L	D

Find the following words from the Scripture reading in the diagram above. Words may appear vertically, horizontally or diagonally.

TIME	SAMUEL	CALLING	SERVANT	STOOD	ELI	LAY
LISTENING	LORD	BED	WENT	SPEAK	DOWN	BOY

Prayer

Dear God,
Thank you that the people who are important to you are the
ones who love you and want to serve you. Thank you for
speaking to Samuel. Help me to be ready to listen and do what
you ask.
In Jesus' name, amen.

Bonus

Ask your parent and a brother, sister or friend to help you act
out the story of Samuel. Choose the part you would like to play
and ask the others to do the other parts (Samuel, Eli and the
voice of God). Samuel will hear God's voice three times. Each
time he will go to Eli, and Eli will tell him to go back to bed.
Finally, when Eli figures out what is happening, he will explain
to Samuel. The next time, Samuel will answer God instead.

9

God Looks at the Inside, Not the Outside

Don't be surprised if your child names a media star rather than someone he or she knows. Because our society values appearance, media "heroes" often capture the imaginations of children. Use the example your child generates and compare this person to Jesse's eldest son later in the lesson.

Sometimes we wish we were like people who are good-looking or athletic or talented. Who do you admire?

When God wanted a new king, he told the prophet Samuel to go to Jesse's house. Samuel was surprised by God's choice.

Bible Reading

[6]When they arrived, Samuel saw Eliab. Samuel thought, "Surely the Lord has appointed this person standing here before him."

[7]But the Lord said to Samuel, "Don't look at how handsome Eliab is. Don't look at how tall he is. I have not chosen him. God does not see the same way people see. People look at the outside of a person, but the Lord looks at the heart." . . .

[10]Jesse had seven of his sons pass by Samuel. But Samuel said to him, "The Lord has not chosen any of these."

[11]Then he asked Jesse, "Are these all the sons you have?"

Jesse answered, "I still have the youngest son. He is out taking care of the sheep."

Samuel said, "Send for him. We will not sit down to eat until he arrives."

¹²So Jesse sent and had his youngest son brought in. He was a fine boy, tanned and handsome.

The Lord said to Samuel, "Go! Appoint him. He is the one." (1 Samuel 16:6-7, 10-12)

Discussion

1. Why did Samuel think that God must have chosen Eliab (verses 6-7)?

2. What did God tell Samuel about the older sons (verse 10)?

3. Why wasn't Jesse's youngest son (David) at home when Samuel came (verse 11)?

3. For something as important as the visit of a prophet, a father would normally gather his whole family. The fact that David stayed with the sheep shows that Jesse also judged from a human perspective. He simply couldn't imagine that the youngest son would be the one that God wanted, especially since age conferred even more status in that society than it does today.

4. What did the Lord tell Samuel about David (verse 12)?

5. What is something special that God sees when he looks at your heart?

5. Help your child to identify a positive character trait. Even if your child is the oldest or only in your family, he or she undoubtedly can think of others who would likely be chosen ahead of him or her, from a human perspective. All of us have times of feeling insignificant or unworthy. It can be good to remind ourselves that God looks on the heart.

✎6. What did Samuel learn about God at Jesse's house?

✎7. What do you think Jesse and his older sons thought when Samuel appointed David as the next king?

Activity

God looks on the inside of us. You will find what God looks at when you color all the areas in the picture that contain a number.

Prayer

Dear God,

Thank you for making me the way you did. Thank you for looking at my heart instead of my appearance. Help me to have a heart that is always ready to serve you.

In Jesus' name, amen.

Bonus

Try an experiment with what is outside a container and what is inside. Find two small objects, one very ordinary (perhaps a penny) and one very special. Wrap them in plain pieces of paper so they look as much the same as possible. Then decorate the package containing the penny so it looks very special. Keep the other package very plain or even ugly. Ask a brother or sister or friend to look at the packages and tell you which is more valuable. Then tell them the story of King David and how God looks at the inside of us.

10

God Has a Purpose for You

Allow your child to answer the question.

Many of the things we own are useful. What are some of the useful things you own? People like to feel useful too. It feels good to be able to help with chores at home, or to help take care of a younger brother or sister.

When you are little, it is sometimes hard to believe that you could have an important purpose for your life. But the Bible says that God was thinking about how you could be useful to him even before you were born.

Bible Reading

[4][Jeremiah said] The Lord spoke these words to me:
  [5]"Before I made you in your mother's womb, I chose you.
  Before you were born, I set you apart for a special work.
  I appointed you as a prophet to the nations."
[6]Then I said, "But Lord God, I don't know how to speak. I am only a boy."
  [7]But the Lord said to me, "Don't say, 'I am only a boy.' You must go everywhere that I send you. You must say everything I tell you to say. [8]Don't be afraid of anyone, because I am with you. I will protect you," says the Lord. (Jeremiah 1:4-8)

Discussion

1. When did God know the purpose for Jeremiah's life (verse 5)?

2. What special purpose did God have for Jeremiah (verse 5)?

3. Why was it hard for Jeremiah to believe that God had a purpose for him (verse 6)?

4. What kinds of people are useful to God?

4. Use this question to help your child expand his or her concept of service to God and his kingdom. If Jeremiah, who felt inadequate because of his youth and inexperience, could have a specially ordained purpose, then your child could as well. Also, people the world tends to view as marginal, such as the poor, the uneducated and the handicapped, each have a unique role in God's plan.

5. How does Jeremiah's story make you glad to be who God made you to be?

✎6. What purpose do you think that God might have for you?

✎7. Why doesn't God use only people who are older and wiser and stronger?

Activity

| a b c d e f g h i j k l m n o p q r s t u v w x y z |

"Epo'u   tbz   J   bn   pomz   b   cpz.

____   ____   __   ____   ____   __   ____ .

Zpv   nvtu   hp   fwfszxifsf   uibu   J

____   ____   ____   _____   ____   _

tfoe   zpv.   Zpv   nvtu   tbz   fwfszuijoh

____   ____ .   ____   ____   ____   _____

J   ufmm   zpv   up   tbz.   Epo'u   cf

_   ____   ____   __   ____ .   ____   __

bgsbje   pg   bozpof,   cfdbvtf   J   bn

____   __   ____ ,   ____   _   ____

xjui   zpv.   J   xjmm   qspufdu   zpv,"

____   ____ .   _   ____   _____   ____ ,"

tbzt   uif   Mpse.

____   ____   _____ .

Use the alphabet to help you decode the paragraph above. Write the correct word in the space below the coded words. Hint: use the letter from the alphabet that comes before the letter provided.

Prayer

Dear God,

Thank you for making me the way you did. Thank you that you have a special purpose for my life. Help me to be ready to be useful to you wherever I am.

In Jesus' name, amen.

Bonus

Find something in your house that isn't very useful. It might be something that you are getting ready to throw away. See if you can think of a new purpose for it. Then, with your parent, thank God that he has a purpose for everything he has made, including you!

11

Allow your child to answer the question.

God Wants You to Learn About Him

People who work as teachers have a very important job. They help children and grownups learn many things. How many teachers do you know? We also learn many things at home from our parents.

The Bible tells us that it is very important for Christian parents to teach their children about God. You are never too young to start learning God's Word. Then, when you are a grownup, you will be able to teach your own children!

Bible Reading

Remember my words in your hearts and souls. Write them down and tie them to your hands as a sign. Tie them on your foreheads to remind you. [19]Teach them well to your children. Talk about them when you sit at home and walk along the road. Talk about them when you lie down and when you get up. [20]Write them on your doors and gates. [21]Then both you and your children will live a long time in the land. This is the land the Lord promised your ancestors. You will live there for as long as the skies are above the earth. (Deuteronomy 11:18-21)

Discussion

1. What does it mean to remember God's words in your heart and soul (verse 18)?

2. When should we talk about God's Word (verse 19)?

3. Why is it a good idea to write down God's words and put them in places where you will see them often (verse 20)?

4. What did God promise to the people of Israel if they would teach their children about him (verse 21)?

5. How does God's Word help you to be happy?

6. What has your parent taught you about God and his Word?

7. Why is it bad when Christians don't talk about God's Word?

7. Whatever is truly important in our lives is a frequent subject of our conversation. Parents naturally want to share with their children the things they value most. If we neglect to talk about God's Word, this is an indication that it has fallen in importance in our lives. If our children see us continually learning about spiritual things, they will be motivated to do likewise.

Activity

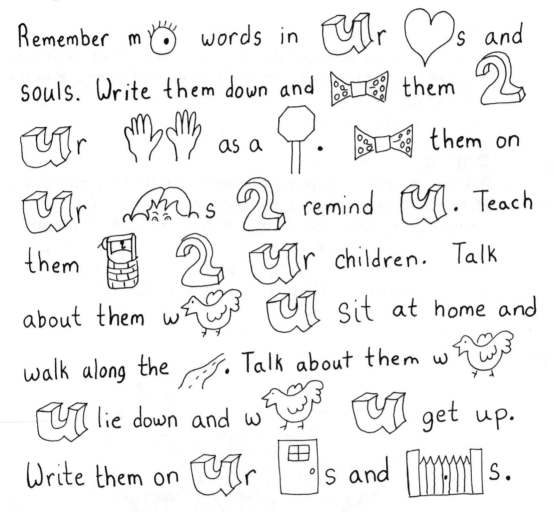

Remember m[eye] words in [U]r [heart]s and souls. Write them down and [bowtie] them [2] [U]r [hands] as a [sign]. [bowtie] them on [U]r [forehead]s [2] remind [U]. Teach them [well] [2] [U]r children. Talk about them w[hen] [U] sit at home and walk along the [road]. Talk about them w[hen] [U] lie down and w[hen] [U] get up. Write them on [U]r [door]s and [gate]s.

This is a portion from the Bible reading with a few changes! Without peeking, try to figure out what the symbols mean.

Prayer

Dear God,

Thank you for making me the way you did. Thank you that you want us to start learning about your Word when we are young children. Help me to keep learning more and more about the Bible all my life.

In Jesus' name, amen.

Bonus

Ask your parent to help you choose a Scripture verse to learn. Have him or her write it at the bottom of a sheet of paper. Then draw a picture that helps you remember the verse and think about what it means. Choose a place (like the refrigerator or your closet door) to hang the picture. When you see it, think about the Scripture. Thank God that he wants all people, especially children, to know him better.

Bible memorization can be an enjoyable experience for children, and you will probably be amazed at their aptitude. You might select some of the passages from this study guide, use a Bible memory system for children, or begin with Exodus 20:1-17, Matthew 5:1-10, or 1 Corinthians 13:1-13.

12

Allow your child to answer the question.

Know Who You Are and Who You Are Not

Dressing up like something or somebody else can be fun. Who have you pretended to be lately? Of course, when you play a game or wear a costume, you still know who you are. And when you stop playing the game, it feels good to act like yourself again.

Sometimes people want others to think they are smarter or more important than they really are. So they pretend all the time. John the Baptist had a chance to do that when people asked him if he was the Savior. But John was glad to be who God had created him to be. He did not pretend.

Bible Reading

²At this time, a command from God came to John son of Zechariah. John was living in the desert. ³He went all over the area around the Jordan River and preached to the people. He preached a baptism of changed hearts and lives for the forgiveness of their sins. . . .

¹⁵All the people were hoping for the Christ to come, and they wondered about John. They thought, "Maybe he is the Christ."

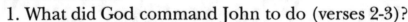

[16]John answered everyone, "I baptize you with water, but there is one coming later who can do more than I can. I am not good enough to untie his sandals. He will baptize you with the Holy Spirit and with fire." (Luke 3:2-3, 15-16)

Discussion

1. What did God command John to do (verses 2-3)?

2. When John baptized people, what were they showing had happened on the inside (verse 3)?

3. What did the people wonder about John the Baptist (verse 15)?

✎4. Why did the people think John might be the Christ (verse 15)?

5. How did John explain the difference between him and Jesus (verse 16)?

✎6. What important job did John the Baptist do for God?

5. John preached repentance to prepare the people for the coming of Christ. If your child is interested, read the entire account of John's ministry together from Luke 3:1-20.

7. Why is it best to be yourself and not pretend to be somebody else?

Activity

The words listed appear in the Bible reading. Use them to complete the crossword.

3 Letters	4 Letters	5 Letters	6 Letters	7 Letters	8 Letters
all	sins	lives	living	command	answered
	good	later	hearts	changed	wondered
			Spirit	sandals	

Prayer

Dear Lord,
Thank you for making me the way you did. Thank you for giving me important work to do. Help me to be happy being the person you made me to be.
In Jesus' name, amen.

Bonus

John the Baptist was glad for the important job God had given him. He did not try to be more important than he was. Think of some of the important jobs God wants you to do for him, even while you are a child. Ask your parent to write them down for you.

13

Jesus Was Once a Child Too

Allow your child to answer the question.

What are some examples of times you have been obedient to your parents? God wants all Christians—children and grown-ups—to obey him. Although Jesus was born into a human family, he was God. He knew many things that the grownup Jewish leaders did not know. Still, he taught us an important lesson by being obedient to Joseph and Mary while he was a boy.

Bible Reading

[43]When the feast days were over, they went home. The boy Jesus stayed behind in Jerusalem, but his parents did not know it. [44]Joseph and Mary traveled for a whole day. They thought that Jesus was with them in the group. Then they began to look for him among their family and friends, [45]but they did not find him. So they went back to Jerusalem to look for him there. [46]After three days they found him. Jesus was sitting in the Temple with the religious teachers, listening to them and asking them questions. [47]All who heard him were amazed at his understanding and wise answers. [48]When Jesus' parents saw him, they were amazed. His mother said to him, "Son why did you do this to us? Your father and I were very worried about you. We have been

looking for you."

⁴⁹Jesus asked, "Why did you have to look for me? You should have known that I must be where my father's work is!" ⁵⁰But they did not understand the meaning of what he said.

⁵¹Jesus went with them to Nazareth and obeyed them. (Luke 2:43-51)

Discussion

1. What did Jesus do when the feast days were over (verse 43)?

2. When did Jesus' parents notice that he was gone (verse 44)?

3. What was Jesus doing when his parents found him (verses 46-47)?

4. Why did it make sense for Jesus to be in the temple talking about God (verse 49)?

✎5. Why were the grownups in this story amazed at the things Jesus said?

✎6. How did Jesus show that he was glad to be who God made him to be (verse 51)?

7. How does Jesus help you to want to obey your parents?

2. You might want to explain to your child that large numbers of relatives and neighbors traveled together from their towns to Jerusalem and back for a major feast. The children of many families would mix together, so it was not unusual for Joseph and Mary to assume that Jesus was somewhere in their group.

7. By being unafraid to discuss religion with the scholars of the day, Jesus showed that he was confident of his identity as God's Son. At the same time, he knew that he was just a boy and the time for his ministry had not yet come. So when his parents didn't understand his actions and worried about him, he was glad to obey them and go back to Nazareth.

Activity

| A B C D E F G H I J K L M N O P |

__ ARENTS

HO __ E

F __ AST

__ OY

FAMI __ Y

W __ TH

S __ N

__ ROUP

B __ CK

A __ TER

AMAZE __

TEA __ HERS

__ OSEPH

T __ REE

BEHI __ D

LOO __

Use the letters above to complete the words that are listed. Hint: All the words above appear in the Bible reading.

Prayer

Dear Jesus,

Thank you for making me the way you did. Thank you for giving me a family. Thank you for showing us the importance of obedience by obeying Mary and Joseph when you were a little boy. Help me to learn obedience so I can better obey God. Amen.

Bonus

When your family is away from home and in crowded places like a mall or busy street, it can be difficult to stay together. With your parent, talk about some good rules for staying together. Also talk about what you should do if you become separated from the rest of your family.

14

God Is at Work in Your Life

When bad things happen to us, we feel very sad. What has made you feel sad lately? Sometimes when bad things happen, it is hard to like being who you are. But even when we are feeling very sad, God is working to bring about something good.

Allow your child to answer the question.

Joseph had something terrible happen to him. His brothers sold him into slavery in Egypt. By the time he met his brothers again, however, he understood how God had been working.

Bible Reading

[4]So Joseph said to them, "Come close to me." So the brothers came close to him. And he said to them, "I am your brother Joseph. You sold me as a slave to go to Egypt. [5]Now don't be worried. Don't be angry with yourselves because you sold me here. God sent me here ahead of you to save people's lives. [6]No food has grown on the land for two years now. And there will be five more years without planting or harvest. [7]So God sent me here ahead of you. This was to make sure you have some descendants left on earth. And it was to keep you alive in an amazing way. [8]So it was not you who sent me here, but God. God has made me the highest officer of the king of Egypt. I am

in charge of his palace. I am the master of all the land of Egypt." (Genesis 45:4-8)

Discussion

1. What secret did the ruler reveal to Joseph's brothers (verse 4)?

2. Why was it good that Joseph already lived in Egypt when his brothers went there for food (verses 5-7)?

3. How did God bless Joseph *and* his brothers?

4. How did God turn the bad thing that happened to Joseph into something good?

5. How does the story of Joseph help you to trust God about bad things that happen to you?

✎6. How do you think Joseph's brothers felt when they found out he was a powerful ruler?

✎7. What bad thing can you ask God to turn into something good in your life?

Activity

Rearrange the words according to the symbols and write them in the blanks provided.

Prayer

Dear God,
Thank you for making me the way you did. Help me to trust you even if bad things happen to me. Please turn the bad things into blessings for many people.
In Jesus' name, amen.

Bonus

Ask your parent to pour water into a glass until the bottom half is full and the top half is empty. Then talk about how you could describe that glass. You will find that there are two ways of looking at the glass. It would be correct to say it is half empty. But it would also be correct to say that it is half full. If you were feeling thirsty, that would be a more positive way to look at the glass of water. Ask God to help you see how he is turning bad things that happen into something good in your life.

Allow your child to answer the questions.

15

Jesus Gives You Strength

Many children like stories about superheroes. When a superhero gets into trouble, he or she can call on some secret source of strength to overcome evil and save the day. Do you like superhero stories? Why or why not?

Of course, we don't know any superheroes in real life. But the apostle Paul said that he had found a source of power that never let him down, no matter what happened to him. Read these verses to find out about the strength Christians have.

Bible Reading

[11]I have learned to be satisfied with the things I have and with everything that happens. [12]I know how to live when I am poor. And I know how to live when I have plenty. I have learned the secret of being happy at any time in everything that happens. I have learned to be happy when I have enough to eat and when I do not have enough to eat. I have learned to be happy when I have all that I need and when I do not have the things I need. [13]I can do all things through Christ because he gives me strength. (Philippians 4:11-13)

Discussion

1. What important lesson did Paul learn (verse 11)?

2. At what surprising times was Paul still able to be happy (verse 12)?

3. What was the source of strength that never let Paul down (verse 13)?

4. What did Paul know he could do with the strength of Christ (verse 13)?

4. Emphasize that Paul was confident that he could do "all things" that God asked him to do. Without this clarification, a child might feel a sense of failure or disappointment at not being able to do everything he or she attempts or wants to do.

5. How can the strength of Christ help you to be happy this week?

✎6. Why is it good to be satisfied with the things we have (verse 11)?

✎7. What makes it possible for Christians to be happy even when bad things happen?

Activity

I CAN DO ALL THINGS

THROUGH CHRIST

BECAUSE HE GIVES

ME STRENGTH.

To complete the sentence above, solve the problems in the key below. Match the number to the letter and write it in the blank provided.

I	M	O	G	E	S	T	R
4+4=	0+1=	13+3=	1+2=	5+4=	2+11=	4+1=	7+5=

H	U	B	N	A	D	V	C
3+1=	12+3=	1+1=	2+4=	6+5=	4+3=	5+5=	3+11=

Prayer

Dear Lord,
Thank you for making me the way you did. Thank you for giving me the strength of Christ. Help me to remember that strength and to trust you in both good times and bad times. In Jesus' name, amen.

Bonus

From some unneeded, old magazines, cut out pictures of people who are either really happy or really sad. Paste the pictures onto a large sheet of paper or cardboard. Explain the pictures to your parent. Ask your parent to write out Philippians 4:13 on your collage. Together, thank God that we have the strength of Christ within us at all times.

Allow your child to answer the question.

16

Your Power Comes from God

Many of us enjoy stories where the smallest, weakest or youngest person wins. Why do you think those stories make people feel good?

The Bible tells us that the world is full of friends of God as well as enemies of God. Sometimes it can seem like the enemies are winning. But the truth is that the enemies have already lost the battle. Read these verses to find out why.

Bible Reading

[1]My dear friends, many false prophets are in the world now. So do not believe every spirit. But test the spirits to see if they are from God. [2]This is how you can know God's Spirit: One spirit says, "I believe that Jesus is the Christ who came to earth and became a man." That Spirit is from God. [3]Another spirit refuses to say this about Jesus. That spirit is not from God but is the spirit of the Enemy of Christ. You have heard that the Enemy of Christ is coming. And now he is already in the world.

[4]My dear children, you belong to God. So you have defeated them because God's Spirit, who is in you, is greater than the devil, who is in the world. (1 John 4:1-4)

Discussion

1. Why should we be careful and not believe people just because they say they are from God (verse 1)?

2. How can we know if someone is a friend of God (verse 2)?

3. How can we know if someone is an enemy of God (verse 3)?

4. What are some ways you can show other people that you belong to God?

5. Why are you glad that God's Spirit in you is greater than the devil?

✎6. Why is it important for Jesus' friends to say that he is the Christ who became a man and died for us and rose again (verse 2)?

✎7. How can we be confident that we have defeated God's enemies (verse 4)?

Activity

grand	ed	send	alliga
est	r's	chum	rself

1. chummy

2. dearest

3. grandchildren

4. yourself

5. belonged

6. alligator's

7. Godsend

Cross out the letters in the numbered words that match the letters in the boxes. Copy the smaller words that remain on the lines that have the same number. You will find a message from the Bible reading.

_____   _____   _____   _____
    1   2   3   4

_____   _____   _____ .
    5   6   7

Prayer

Dear God,
Thank you for making me the way you did. Thank you that I belong to you. Thank you that I am strong enough to defeat your enemies because your Spirit lives inside of me.
In Jesus' name, amen.

Bonus

You know that in a game of tug-of-war, the stronger person always wins. Play a game of tug-of-war with your parent. Then imagine playing this game with someone much smaller than you, such as a baby. Together take time to thank God that Jesus is much stronger than his enemy, the devil. Thank God that Jesus always wins against the devil. Thank him that Jesus has already won and that he lives in us.

You Can Serve God

Allow your child to answer the question.

It can be fun to know someone who is very, very good at something. It can also be difficult to know that person. You might sometimes feel bad because you cannot do the same thing. Which of your friends is very good at something?

God made each of us, and he knows that we are not all good at the same things. But the Bible teaches that every Christian is good at something. It is that way so we can help each other.

Bible Reading

⁴There are different kinds of gifts; but they are all from the same Spirit. ⁵There are different ways to serve; but all these ways are from the same Lord. ⁶And there are different ways that God works in people; but all these ways are from the same God. God works in us all in everything we do. ⁷Something from the Spirit can be seen in each person, to help everyone. ⁸The Spirit gives one person the ability to speak with wisdom. And the same Spirit gives another the ability to speak with knowledge. ⁹The same Spirit gives faith to one person. And that one Spirit gives another gifts of healing. ¹⁰The Spirit gives to another person the power to do miracles, to another the ability to prophesy. And

he gives to another the ability to know the difference between good and evil spirits. The Spirit gives one person the ability to speak in different kinds of languages and to another the ability to interpret those languages. [11]One Spirit, the same Spirit, does all these things. (1 Corinthians 12:4-11)

Discussion

1. Where do we get our abilities to serve each other (verses 4-5)?

2. Why did God see to it each person has some gift (verse 7)?

3. What kinds of abilities does the Holy Spirit give to Christians (verses 8-10)?

✎4. Why is it good that God doesn't give the same gift to every person?

5. Your child is probably not in a position to understand and identify spiritual gifts in the same way an adult would approach the subject. However, you may be surprised that he or she can tell you about some kind of service that comes naturally or feels good. If necessary, help your child name one ability by naming a few of the things you have seen him or her do for others.

5. Who decides what gift to give each person (verse 11)?

6. What gift has God given you so you can serve other people?

✎7. How can knowing that God's Spirit gives you special abilities help you to be glad to be the person God made you?

Activity

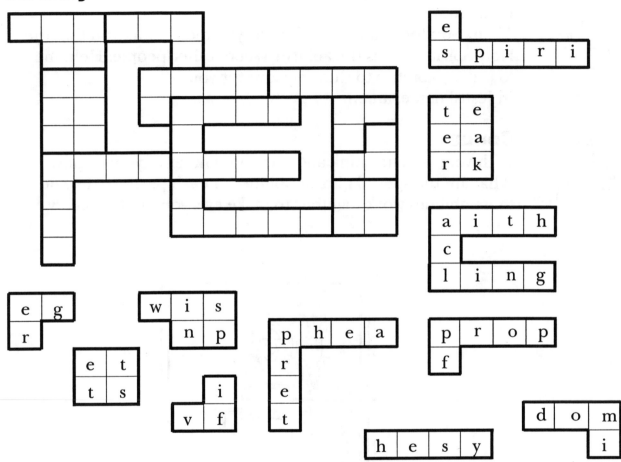

Use the pieces to complete the puzzle. Write the letters in the spaces that match the shapes. When you have filled in the letters, try to find the words below from the Bible reading.

spirit	speak	faith	wisdom	serve
healing	interpret	miracles	gifts	prophesy

Prayer

Dear God,
Thank you for making me the way you did. Thank you that the Holy Spirit gives us the ability to serve other people. Help me to use my abilities to show my love for you.
In Jesus' name, amen.

Bonus

With your parent, think about each member of your family. What are the special gifts or abilities of each person? How do those abilities work together to make everyone in the family happier?

18

You Have Something Better Than Money

Most of us wish we had more money. We can think of many things we'd like to do with that money. What do you wish you had enough money to buy?

The Bible teaches that if we spend all our time thinking about getting more things and more money, we will actually be unhappy. You can make yourself miserable thinking about all the things you *don't* have. Read the following verses to see why Christians have a special reason to be happy.

Bible Reading

[5]Keep your lives free from the love of money. And be satisfied with what you have. God has said,

"I will never leave you;
I will never forget you."
[6]So we can feel sure and say,
"I will not be afraid because the Lord is my helper.
People can't do anything to me." (Hebrews 13:5-6)

Discussion

1. What does the Bible teach us to feel about the things we have (verse 5)?

2. Why is it harder to love God if we are always thinking about money?

3. What wonderful promise has God made to Christians (verse 5)?

4. How do some people try to use money to keep them safe?

5. Why don't you need to depend on money for your safety if you are a Christian (verse 6)?

6. Older children will certainly recognize that people can, and do, do terrible things to one another. However, they can also be introduced to the concept that our eternal souls belong to God. No matter what happens to our bodies or our possessions, no human being has the power to take away our salvation.

✎6. What does the Bible mean when it says, "People can't do anything to me" (verse 6)?

✎7. How is it possible to *have* money without *loving* it too much?

Activity

love	hungry	
medicine	thirsty	
fan	tired	
sleep	cold	
food	hot	
blanket	sick	
water	sad	

God wants us to be satisfied with what we have. In the middle are feelings and needs we have. Find the thing on the left that will satisfy each need. Write the word in the box.

Prayer

Dear God,

Thank you for making me the way you did. Thank you for promising that you will never leave me or forget me. Please keep me from loving money too much. Help me to trust you for the things that I need.

In Jesus' name, amen.

Bonus

Try this activity to help you be satisfied with what you have. Think of your top ten favorite possessions. Ask your parent to write down your list for you. At your next prayer time, use the list to thank God for all the good things he has given you.